Popular Ballads for Classical Singers

Low Voice

Concert Arrangements by Richard Walters

Contents

RICHARD RODGERS
4   The Sweetest Sounds *(lyric by the composer)*
11   I Have Dreamed *(lyric by Oscar Hammerstein II)*
19   You're Nearer *(lyric by Lorenz Hart)*

COLE PORTER
lyrics by the composer
24   I Am in Love
33   I Concentrate on You
43   I Hate You, Darling

GEORGE GERSHWIN
lyrics by Ira Gershwin
48   They Can't Take That Away from Me
57   Nice Work If You Can Get It
65   A Foggy Day/Love Walked In
74   Love Is Here to Stay

On the cover: Wassily Kandinsky, *Round and Pointed,* 1930

ISBN 0-634-02304-7

HAL•LEONARD®
CORPORATION
7777 W. BLUEMOUND RD. P.O. BOX 13819 MILWAUKEE, WI 53213

Visit Hal Leonard Online at
www.halleonard.com

Arranger's Notes

Among the most fascinating characteristics of standard American popular songs is their amazing ability to retain a distinct identity in a wide spectrum of arranging styles. For this collection I have chosen songs for which I could make appropriate concert settings designed to flatter classical singers and pianists. These are more in the spirit of classical compositions based on the songs, rather than typical arranging.

THE SWEETEST SOUNDS comes from the 1962 musical *No Strings*, a gentle interracial romance that starred Diahann Carroll and Richard Kiley. It was the composer's first stage work after the death in 1960 of his partner, Oscar Hammerstein II, and is the only show in Rodgers' long career for which he wrote his own lyrics. In this instance, the imagery of the words seem to reveal the self-intimacy between Rodgers the lyricist and Rodgers the composer. The result is an unusually chromatic and haunting melody.

I HAVE DREAMED is the famous love duet sung by Tuptim and Lun Tha in the 1951 Rodgers and Hammerstein musical *The King and I*. This love song, sung by two people who have not yet actually become lovers, has similar counterparts in other shows, for instance, "People Will Say We're in Love" from *Oklahoma!*, "If I Loved You" from *Carousel*, "Some Enchanted Evening" from *The King and I*, or even Hammerstein's earlier work in "Make Believe" from *Show Boat*. "I Have Dreamed" is the kind of sweeping, idealized, romantic song that is at the heart of the Rodgers and Hammerstein output. The arrangement is designed to start with a wispy, tenuous notion, then a tender romantic vision, progressing to full-blown operatic passion.

YOU'RE NEARER is one of Lorenz Hart's typically expressive lyrics in his collaborations with Richard Rodgers. The song was added to the 1940 movie version of the 1939 Rodgers and Hart musical *Too Many Girls*, and was later included in the 1959 revised stage version of *Babes and Arms*. Hart combines genuinely lyrical ideas—"Dearer than the rain is to the earth below, precious as the sun to the things that grow"—with the light touch that keeps the sentiments sincere, but witty, modern and casual, in lines such as "nearer than the ivy to the wall is." I call such spots in American standards "smile lines." Most present day artists sing standards far too earnestly, and miss the playful casual wit found even in the best love songs of the 1920s to mid-1950s. The high point of "You're Nearer" strays furthest away, at the words "Leave me." My arrangement was inspired by Judy Garland's performance on her album "Live at Carnegie Hall," accompanied in a lovely, simple arrangement.

I AM IN LOVE, from the 1953 musical *Can-Can*, is a good example of literate wit mixed with sex that is so typical of many of Cole Porter's lighter love songs. There also seems to be a strong French connection in Porter's material. Five of his Broadway scores, including *Can-Can*, are set in Paris, along with a couple of film scores, and Porter spent a good bit of his life there. A hot, debonaire, urbane Parisian attitude about romance figures into the pallet. This song illustrates the seemingly effortless play of a brilliant creative mind, and I have tried to capture the fun of the song in my arrangement. I can recommend trying some kind of thick, broad French or Italian accent for the repeat of the "bridge" (at the words "I knew the gods were against me…"), snapping out of the accent at "I may lose, but I refuse…"

I CONCENTRATE ON YOU, written for the movie *Broadway Melody of 1940*, was known to me for many years primarily through Frank Sinatra's breezy swing recording from the 1950s. It wasn't until I heard other singers' renditions (Ella Fitzgerald most significantly) that I realized that this is one of the straight-faced love ballads by Cole Porter. The songwriter was able to come up with clever and witty songs fairly easily, but by all accounts, longed most to write powerfully memorable, heartfelt love songs such as Berlin's "What'll I Do?" or "Always."

I HATE YOU, DARLING is from Cole Porter's 1941 show *Let's Face It*. It was originally performed in a quiet and romantic style, making an ironic contrast with the lyrics. I heard the hint of darker emotions in the tune and words, and decided to do a setting taking the love/hate emotions of the song more literally. There is a more explicit reference to sex and relationships in Cole Porter songs than in the work of any other songwriters of the era. Running with that spirit, I stretched the subtext, arranging it as a world-weary Berlin ballad, modeled after Brecht and Weill, where the singer self-mockingly reveals his/her self-destructive liason with someone of inescapable lure.

THEY CAN'T TAKE THAT AWAY FROM ME is one of several songs the Gershwin brothers wrote for Fred Astaire, this one for the 1937 film *Shall We Dance*. It's tucked into the movie in an understated scene on board the Staten Island Ferry, sung once through to Ginger Rogers, without reprise or dancing. The subject is a sophisticated, civil end to romance, and I have tried to evoke that sad nostalgia in the arrangement. Believe it or not, I used sections of *Der Rosenkavalier* as a musical inspiration. Then there is a mid-song shift to a swing style that is an extroverted re-enactment of the romance's bright moments, spilling into a hint of bitterness and desperation ("The way you hold your knife"), concluding with a return to the nostalgia of the opening.

NICE WORK IF YOU CAN GET IT, like all the Gershwin songs in this collection, is from the brothers' late Hollywood work of 1937. This one comes from another Fred Astaire picture, *A Damsel in Distress, sans* Ginger Rogers. Like some of the best lyrics of the late 1930s, this song primarily presents a casual view of romance that masks inner earnest longing. The aesthetics of the best popular music of the era leaned toward a distinctly American style that valued a literate wit, gentle self-deprecation, concealment of effort, indirect references, avoidance of seriousness but with sincere underlying intent, and intelligence expressed in vernacular slang. In this arrangement I have attempted to contrast the dreamy lines with the more rhythmic realism of the song's title phrase. The concealed loneliness and longing emerges at the end in an "emotional coda."

A FOGGY DAY/LOVE WALKED IN. "A Foggy Day," another Fred Astaire song, was written for the 1937 movie *A Damsel in Distress*. In a mere two minutes, the song paints a detailed picture of a lonely American in London (it never states he's an American, but we know it by implication and style), weary of sightseeing, absently roaming the strange city in a grey mood to match the foggy streets. Suddenly and unexpectedly he turns the corner to find love and romance. It's a stunning song. "Love Walked In" was written for the 1937 movie *The Goldwyn Follies*, George Gershwin's last project, sung by by the sweet "lunch counter tenor" of Kenny Baker. I heard the similar sentiments of the two songs, and felt they would comment upon one another if combined in an arrangement.

LOVE IS HERE TO STAY, from the movie *The Goldwyn Follies*, is the last song the Gershwin brothers wrote together, and they certainly never wrote a better popular song. It's intelligent, urbane, casual, witty, undeniably American, and truly romantic—a jewel-like souvenir from 1937 that perfectly represents is era and yet has a timelessness about it. The song is a masterpiece of its style and, in my opinion, has few peers among romantic American ballads.

THE SWEETEST SOUNDS

Lyrics and Music by Richard Rodgers
Arranged by Richard Walters

6

ev - er know   Are wait - ing

to be said. _____ The

most en - tranc - ing sight of all   Is

yet for me to see. _____

The kind - est words I'll ev - er

know   Are   wait - ing   to   be   said. _____

The   most   en - tranc - ing   sight   of

all   Is   yet   for   me   to   see. _____

And   the   dear - est   love   in   all   the

I HAVE DREAMED

Words by Oscar Hammerstein II
Music by Richard Rodgers
Arranged by Richard Walters

♩ = c. 80-84

too._____ I have dreamed_____

that your arms are love - ly,

I have dreamed _____ what a joy you'll be.

I have dreamed _____ ev -'ry word you'll

and en - joyed the view. In these

dreams I've loved you so That by now I think I

know What it's like to be loved by

you, I will

love   be - ing   loved   by   you.

I   have dreamed _____ ev -'ry word   you'll __

whis - per When you're ___ close,

close to ___ me. ___

cresc.

How you look ___ in the glow of ___ eve -

loco

romantically; *think Rachmaninoff in this section*

- ning, I have dreamed, ___

love   be - ing   loved   by _____ you. _____

YOU'RE NEARER

Words by Lorenz Hart
Music by Richard Rodgers
Arranged by Richard Walters

Leave me, but when you're a - way You'll

know _____ you're ___ near - er, _____

for I love you so. _____

I AM IN LOVE

Words and Music by Cole Porter
Arranged by Richard Walters

la - tion _ mixed with de - fla - tion? _

What ex - pla - na - tion? _

I _ am in

love!

Such con-flict - ing ques - tions ride

a - round in my brain.

Should I or - der

cy - a - nide   or   or - der cham - pagne?

Oh,   what   is   this   sud - den   jolt?_   I   feel   like   a

fright - ened   colt _   just   hit   by   a   thun - der - bolt;_

I   am   in   love!   I

29

for flam - ing de - sire, But

since the gods _____ gave me you to a - dore,

I may lose, but I re - fuse to fight the

cresc.

molto _rit._ _rit._

fire! _____ So,

_f_ _molto_ _rit._ _colla voce_

Tempo Primo

come and __ en - light-en my days and nev - er de -

part. You on - ly can bright-en the blaze __

__ that burns in my heart, For I am

wild - ly in love with you and so in

need of ___ a stam - pede of ___ love! ___

rhythmically

mf

And so in

need of ___ a stam - pede of ___ love! ___

rhythmically   cresc.

p

f secco

press to the end

no rit.

8 - ♩

I CONCENTRATE ON YOU

Words and Music by Cole Porter
Arranged by Richard Walters

When - ev - er skies look grey to me _____ And trou - ble be - gins to brew, _____

When - ev - er the win - ter winds_____ be - come too

strong. I con - cen - trate on _____

you. _____

When for - tune cries "nay, nay!" to me _____

36

On your smile so sweet, so ten - der, _____ When at first *{ my kiss you de - cline, / your kiss I de - cline, } On the light in your eyes, When {you / I} sur -

* Traditionally, women sing "your kiss I decline."

ren - der And once a - gain our

arms in - ter - twine. _____

And so when wise men say to me _____

_____ That love's young dream nev - er comes

38

* *This spot might work better for some singers as a subito forte.*

I con - cen -trate _____ _____ and
con - cen - trate _____ _____ on you. _____

pp

pp

I HATE YOU, DARLING

Words and Music by Cole Porter
Arranged by Richard Walters

Slow Two, "Weillish"

I hate you, dar-ling, my tur-tle dove,_

I hate you, dar-ling, all else a-bove_

I hate you, dar-ling, Be-cause I love_

you so.

I should be clev - er and say "good - bye,"

Good - bye, for - ev - er, my but-ter - fly.

But why be clev - er When dar-ling I

need the joy you bring— more than an - y - thing— I

know. I'm in the depths of _____ In -

fer - no _____ When you're far a - way _____ from me,

dear, _____ But when our sweet nights _____ re -

*Fall off the note.

THEY CAN'T TAKE THAT AWAY FROM ME

Words by Ira Gershwin
Music by George Gershwin
Arranged by Richard Walters

Our ro-mance won't end on a sor-row-ful

note, Though by to-mor-row you're gone; The

song is end - ed, but as the song - writ - er wrote, The

mel - o - dy ___ lin - gers on. They may take you from

me, I'll miss your fond ca - ress. But

though they take you from me, I'll still pos - sess:

50

*These optional notes may be played to support the singer's entrances.

52

No, __ no! __ They can't __ take that a-way from me. We may

Faster and freely, parlando
Swing beat stops, straight eighths

nev - er, nev - er meet a - gain on the bump - y road to

NICE WORK IF YOU CAN GET IT

Words by Ira Gershwin
Music by George Gershwin
Arranged by Richard Walters

The man who on-ly lives for mak-ing mon-ey Lives a life that is-n't nec-es-sa-ri-ly sun-ny. Like-wise the man who works for fame, There's no guar-an-tee that time won't e-rase his name.

58

The fact is, the on-ly work that real-ly brings en-joy-ment

Is the kind that is for girl and boy meant, Fall in love you

won't re-gret it, That's the best work of all ___ if you can

get it.

get it if __ you try.__ Just im - ag - ine

some - one __ Wait - ing at the cot - tage door, __

Where two hearts be - come one __ Who could ask for an - y -thing more?_

Lov - ing one who loves you, And then tak - ing that

* ad lib.

N

Nice work__ if you can   get it,   And you can

* The singer may improvise any syllables to create the dreamy effect if a hum is not preferred.

get it if ___ you try. ___ Just im - ag - ine

some - one, ___ Wait - ing at the cot-tage door, ___

Where two hearts be - come one ___ Who could ask for an -

- y - thing more? Lov - ing one who loves you, ___

And then tak - ing that vow,

Nice work if you can get it,

And if you get it, Won't *Opt.* you tell ___ me

how?

quick to the end

A FOGGY DAY/LOVE WALKED IN

Words by Ira Gershwin
Music by George Gershwin
Arranged by Richard Walters

Moderately slow, with freedom

casually espressivo

I was a strang-er in the cit - y. Out of town were the peo-ple I knew. I had that feel-ing of self pit - y, What to do? What to do? What to do? The out-look was de-cid - ed - ly

66

had me down. ___   I viewed the morn - ing

with a - larm, ___ The Brit - ish Mu - se - um had

lost its charm. ___ How long, I won - dered, could

this thing last? ___ But the age of mir - a - cles

Some singers may be more comfortable with a forte here.

walked right in and drove the shad-ows a-way;

Love walked right in and brought my sun-ni-est day.

One mag-ic mo-ment and my heart seemed to know That love said "Hello," Though not a word was spo - ken. One

look and I for - got the gloom of the past;

One look and I had found my fu - ture at

last. One look and I had found a world

com - plete - ly new, When love walked in with

you. _____

One mag - ic mo - ment

and my heart seemed to know   That love said "Hel-

lo,"   Though not a word was spo-ken.

gently   *opt.*

rit.

a tempo
mf

One   look and I for-got the gloom of the past;

One   look and I had found my fu-ture at last.

rit.
cresc.

*Expressively fall off the note.

LOVE IS HERE TO STAY

Words by Ira Gershwin
Music by George Gershwin
Arranged by Richard Walters

way.

In time the Rock-ies may crum-ble, Gi-

bral-ter may tum-ble, They're on-ly made of clay, But

our love is here to stay.

A little freely and faster, parlando

The more I read the pa-pers, The less I com-pre-hend The

world and all its ca - pers, And how it all will end.

Noth - ing seems to be last - ing, But that is - n't our af - fair;

We've got some - thing per - ma - nent, I mean in the way we

care. It's ver - y clear